the three o'clock
in the morning sessions

angie martin

This edition published by Angie Martin
Text © Angie Martin 2014
ISBN-10: 1535154101
ISBN-13: 978-1535154109

Cover Art by: Novak Illustration

To learn more about author Angie Martin, visit her website at
http://www.angiemartinbooks.com/

This work of fiction contains adult situations that may not be suitable for children under eighteen years of age. Recommended for mature audiences only.

novels by angie martin

False Security

Conduit

The Boys Club

dedication

for all the broken hearts out there. they won't stay broken forever.

what are the three o'clock in the morning sessions?

the three o'clock in the morning sessions are the times when you feel most alone
when you sit by yourself, wishing someone was next to you
when you can't sleep, you can't dream
comfort is nowhere to be found

the room is filled with might-have-beens
your heart is full of sorrow
your mind is full of wisdom that you wasted on something else
and there are no more tomorrows

the three o'clock in the morning sessions are filled with heartache
with loss, with pain
with soulful crying outs and never-ending tears
life is all in lowercase, and so are you

it is the time your heart beats for someone not there
when you wish you had done things differently
a time filled with melancholy memories
when you wish you weren't you

everyone's three o'clock in the morning sessions are just a little different
here are mine

patience

there he sits
sits and waits
holding still
for a twist of fate
in a crowded room
far away
will he see me
this lonely day

he turns his head
and i can't believe
his eyes are looking
right past me
this invisible girl
with an invisible heart
slowly shattering
into a thousand parts

but the music playing
from his eyes
encompasses me
goes deep inside
raptures my soul
in a symphony
until i can
no longer see me

should i do it

part my lips
open my heart
let the words slip
out of the mouth
that longs to taste
savor his love
not one moment waste

it isn't right
it isn't fair
why i should feel
why i should care
about this man
who does not see
about this man
lord, set me free

and so like he
i'll sit and wait
holding still
for a twist of fate
patience till
i find my way
patience till
my dying day

after the fall

there are moments in time
when i don't feel so alone
looking over my shoulder
to see where it all began
how you could have known
to find me when i was so lost

i long for you to reach for me
hold my heart in your hands
fill this void with something
only you possess
undress my soul with desire
that cannot be contained

an erupting passion
never to be controlled
a gentle touch from behind
a wistful smile, and a dream
that melodic voice moving me
to the ends of the earth

breaking up my rain clouds
with the light of desire
all those unspoken words
suddenly expressed in a touch
emotions swell from
an intense memory

i free my soul
and close my eyes
you're all that's there
that's all that i see
everything i am
i breathe into you

the box

shhh
come here
just a little closer
i have a secret to show you
but you already know that
don't you?
no matter
i'll still show you
but you have to

come here
and promise to not tell a soul
we'll dig it out
of this dusty, cobwebbed box
now don't worry about me
i trust your intentions are good
i knew it when i first saw you
that curious innocence
dancing in your eyes

yes, i saw that as well
there's a lot that i saw
things that i could never tell you
but you already know that, too
don't you?
no matter
my secret's the important thing

the box seems bottomless, i know
but please bear with me
oh, ignore that skeleton there
we'll just toss it aside
it's only there to scare people
what, you're not scared?
neither am i
at least not anymore

yes, there was a time
when the dark kept coming
but no longer
wait, there it is
the secret i wanted to show you
i realize it's simple
only a mirror
yet if you hold it up
then you'll understand

reckless

standing eagerly
on the edge of life
under a full moon
devouring all inhibition

a sensual song
caressing my skin
like an arousing touch
awakening my body

a heated dance of need
stealing breath from my lungs
succumbing to the ecstasy
bendable and breakable

a feverish crescendo
building upon my mind
leaving red marks of passion
burning upon my soul

the sweet taste of intensity
leaving bitterness on my tongue
endless tears of desire
scraping across my thoughts

pushing the limits
but no longer caring

going zero to nowhere
reckless with my heart

whispers

whispers
of summer storms
thunders crashing
raindrops invigorating

whispers
of daylight dreams
images flourishing
colors merging

whispers
of silent songs
melodies promising
passions escalating

whispers
of provocative pulses
hearts trembling
souls capturing

whispers of touch
moving along the seas
whispers of taste
setting the world free
whispers of time
casually falling over me

whispers
of missed memories
storms unshaped
dreams unimagined

whispers
of tangled truths
songs unheard
pulses untouched

whispers
of you

why

why did you break my heart
and not her heart
or hers over there

what drew you my way
to my weakness
my stupidity

when did you decide
to pull me in
and cause me pain

how was i different
that you'd want to
hurt only me

who are you to do this
to an innocent
who loved you so

why did you break my heart
and not her heart
or hers over there

the offbeat poem

i listen to the world
as it moves
andante

while my heart
is beating
presto alla tedesca

completely offbeat
although
every now and again

the rhythm slows down
only to find
you

and i wonder why
the tears are jerked
from my soul

as i casually allow myself
to drop an inch
or even two

maybe i simply don't see
what everyone else
clearly sees

or maybe
i saw
what no one else could

when i looked up and found
the truth of inner beauty
but now i feel

so ugly outside
that the reflection of me
is repulsive

and i wonder what
you see
if you ever look at me

maybe

night falls uncomfortably
stars explode one by one
and the moon flees my sight
clinging to scraps of hope
and mountains of sacrificed love
a numb haze cyclones around me

i dream of the spring i once knew
and light i thought would always be
a smile arising from a memory
and a hand touching, reassuring
a sweet, pure, gentle kiss
tasting so ripe, so perfectly right
sensation that strips away every fear

when i wake the light remains
smothered with darkness
i shudder as hope threatens to choke
there's nothing left to do but
close my eyes and allow
a little light to shine through
because maybe, just maybe

darkness

i open my eyes to total darkness
a shape before me
hovering over me
the welcomed pain striking
blinding
fingers tracing, intoxicating
an insatiable craving
beating through my skin
the ever-desirable hunger
feed it, please it
sustain the feeling inside
growing beyond its boundaries
that heat which needs the sun
spilling over
an intertwining sharing
swirling down the black hole
completely swallowing
everything there is
always open for you
steal the essence of me
that silhouette before me
reveling in darkness
don't show me the light

one person

just one person
trying to stand out
in a world filled
with one persons

bogged down
by fears of the past
pushed back
by memories of the future

wishing for a face
no one knows
and a name
no one can forget

imagining a life
with nothing but easy
but still desiring
to fight my way through

screaming with
a need to fly
exploding with
the pain of passion

savoring the taste of skin
that lingers on my fingertips

yet desperately ignoring
the magic of that touch

falling in love
with the idea of nothing
always remembering
how it never was

hoping to be someone
to somebody
when everyone
is nobody special

just one person
dreaming an everlasting dream
and wanting nothing more
than to not want

vast stupidity

nothing is greater
than the anger held
in the confines
of a broken heart

a wasted love
forever forsaken
standing directly
in front of you

in desperate need
of a rescue
reaching and grasping
for the impossible

is stupidity so vast
that one cannot see
the truth shining
all around them

blind dreams
that never see light
waking to the nightmare
of realism in you

the destroyer of
perfection

bleeds green
from that broken heart

it never mends
it never dries
the burning tears
dead to life

laughing in unison
the melodies of pity
faded memories
of the one held before you

gone
stolen in time
stupidity erased
the one true to you

rain

water caresses the earth
spilling from the sky tenderly
nature's songs serenade the
world through an
open window
the unspoiled smell of rain

invading the
perfect night

hands grasp my cool skin
then slowly release
tingling my body
rousing that dormant
side of me
a beautiful face

hovers, waiting
watching

i push you away and
rise to meet you
my mouth aching
longing
to taste you
grab the back of your head

my naked body
arches into yours

lines awaken the
liveliness in your eyes
as a smile filled with
love dances on your mouth
rain teases my ears
your breath warm on my face

tears well
filling the moment

my eyes fling open
still wet with tears
choking me alone in silence
except for the sound of rain
in bed with thoughts of you
alone in the dark of life

wondering
if it rains in your world, too

moments

there are moments by myself
when i feel so alone
constantly looking over my shoulder
to see where it all began
i long for you to reach for me
hold my heart in your hands
fill this void with something
desire greater than the body can contain
thoughts the mind can no longer control

and still…

there are moments by myself
when i don't feel so alone
constantly looking beyond this path
to see where it all will lead
i long for you to reach for me
holding time in your hands
burning intensely with hopes of love
twisted time and forgotten days
the tomorrow of today's beginnings

and yet…

there is a moment
when i will not be alone
the breath of passion on parted lips

aching with anxious desire
staring into the depths of a soul
reflected onto my own eyes
and the world simply stops
in that whispered instant
just before your kiss

before the moon disappears

before the moon disappears
step out into the night
stare up at the sky and see
the wind carries behind the clouds
whistling with the hope of dreams

close your eyes and shut out
this life, this night
do you feel me; hear my
translucent thoughts drifting along
the delicate curves of the night

far beyond any normal reach
but very much within your touch
believing that once again it might smile
look into eyes ripe with need
before the moon disappears

tainted

why do you float through my thoughts
coming in and out of my life
unwelcome and uninvited
avoiding the destruction of time
memories misleading with false hopes
and why do you haunt me now
draining my desire to care
leaving me numb and bent
falling down in front of the world
holding onto broken dreams
what wouldn't i give to hear your voice
to know you are thinking of me tonight
sometimes we have to lie to ourselves
if we're to survive the days

awakening

the dream did not end the way i imagined
it started out quite different as well
but life is such that i paid it no heed
and continued down the stubborn path
i woke up on the side of the road
strife flowing through veins of lead
wondering how i ended up in the place
where pain and pleasure are equated
as feelings of life, as feelings of love
nothing more than a defunct kind of lie
driving my soul to disastrous fate
and now that i think about it
if i could choose my perfect ending
would it be you
a laugh escapes my tired lips
and my chafed heart suddenly warms
because i remember that one day
you get to wake up, too

the door

What the hell am I doing? This isn't me, hasn't been for a few years. I keep to myself, keep a strict schedule. Wake up at 6:30 every morning, eat Lucky Charms, take a shower. Drive to work, sit in a cubicle all day, eat lunch at my desk. Leave work at 5:00 each day, sometimes 5:01, if I'm feeling generous. Sit in rush hour traffic, sing along to the radio, occasionally cuss out another driver in a "who-cut-off-who" disagreement. Get home, feed the cat, cook my dinner—usually something simple. Do the dishes, watch my recorded programs, maybe call Mom, if I'm feeling generous. Take another shower, put on frumpy but comfy pajamas, and go to bed.

That's it. There's no time for anything else. Not even on weekends. I'm much too busy playing with Kitty and playing offline solitaire to partake in outside activities.

So what am I doing, sitting in my car, looking at this restaurant, wondering what horrors await me? I haven't eaten out in years. I squint my eyes and spot the large, blue "A" by the front door. Who knows when the health inspector was there last? Surely there are cockroaches in the kitchen, mold in the pantry. The chicken is undercooked and I will get food poisoning. I'll vomit out my internal organs and have to go to the hospital, quite possibly to die of some strange, rare disease that I contract.

That's not true, I know. It's nice to think like that. It makes it easier to try to convince myself to turn the ignition back on and drive away, screeching my tires like I'm late for the racetrack. The car key stays in my purse, though. It doesn't want to jump back into the slot for which it was created.

What the hell happened?

This isn't me, hasn't been for a few years. I keep to myself, keep myself locked up tight. I only speak when spoken to, I never state an opinion. I don't think anyone at work knows anything about me except my name, maybe my job title. I might offer up a question of how someone is doing, if I'm feeling generous. I don't dare approach the "what-did-you-do-this-weekend" question, even if I'm feeling generous.

That's it. There's no room for anything else. Not even when the new guy at work decides to talk to me. I'm much too introverted to even possibly think he's cute, which he's not. He's gorgeous.

So what happened, that I'm sitting in my car, knowing he's in the restaurant, wondering where I am? I'm late, just a few minutes late right now, but if I sit here much longer, he might think I've stood him up. But if I go in there, if I dare to slide out of my car and approach the front door, if I slip into the booth across from him and start to get to know him, start to let him know me, then I might just end up with a broken heart.

That's not true, I know. At least I have no reason to believe it just yet. I simply can't face the idea of swinging open the door to my heart. It's already been cracked, just a little, by his eyes, by his voice. I didn't even know he had the key. I threw it away a few years ago and I never made a duplicate.

I take one last look in the rearview mirror, make sure no ugliness is too apparent on my face, grab my purse, and open the car door. My heart jumps into my throat and I shut the door, forcing my feet to move in the general direction of the restaurant, in the general direction of him. I may get food poisoning, I may get my heart broken. And I'm not even feeling generous.

What the hell am I doing?

magic

there's a certain magic
a spell cast over
the unsuspecting
in the pause of life
i knew better
i knew what to look for
but mistakes are made
in moments of weak souls
regret becoming the muse
of my darkest days

and i wonder
who will save me

so i withdraw
back into my world
and choke back the words
ignore the thoughts
take back that kiss you stole
along with the light
from my eyes
but there's a certain magic
a spell cast over
the unsuspecting

and i wonder
how i will survive it

more darkness

darkness descends behind my eyes
i see that you are waiting
my soul is open tonight
and my smile fills the earth
do you hear the music in my head
feel what i see when you
touch my world, bring it alive
i tear it down, it's all down
and what is it that you see
every time you look straight through
or do you see past everything
staring into the darkness

maybe tomorrow in my
broken down, worn down world
i'll use that strength that pulls you
and let you really feel me
let your smile envelop my soul
before i fall apart
feel me, free me
tear it down, it's all down
give me something to hold onto
before i beat you with your obscurities
imprint me on your soul
never let me go

did you ever

did you ever whisper hello
and open someone's tomorrow

did you ever smile wistfully
and spark a soul to blaze

did you ever share a secret
and intoxicate a stained mind

did you ever soften your touch
and tempt a sensual encounter

did you ever simply live your life
and cause an endless hunger

did you ever walk into a room
and force a heart to love

or would it matter in the least
if you knew you now have

nameless

you ask me what was his name
who was it that put me where i am
the name doesn't matter, but if you insist
his name was *****

you want me to answer questions
tell you how i feel
tell you what i see every time
i see you standing there

why does it matter so much to you
you shouldn't care, not about me
the nameless one, who flutters about
holding onto lost dreams

you won't get your answers
i would never let those secrets out
and before you know it one day, someday
you might just be the nameless one

the angel

a city
dark and desolate
trees stand still
in a windless time
barest of branches
reaching for no one
covered by a shadow

large wings
embrace the earth
swooping down
it is the abandoned one
falling from the sky
through the darkest
night of nights

the angel flies
the angel cries
in search of hope
in search of life
reaching for something
she tumbles down
down, down, down

but then stands tall
before the city
decrepit and destroyed

the angel screams
not with pain, but with joy
she has found her home
she has found her home

fade away

if i sit very still
quiet, holding my breath
if i stop time
with my mind
slow the beating of my heart

will you fade away
into the deepest of dark
just as your face leaves me
with the dawning of the light
leaving me alone to drown

will you ever have the need
to come to me
catch me in the
cascade of tears
filling this voided life

and if i had known
that night was the last
would i have kissed you
just a little differently
savored your mouth

and stolen you from the world
held you as tenderly
as breaking glass

crashing into what
tomorrow brings

doesn't seem to matter
not in the depths of the lonely
night falling on this soul
broken once more as the days
seem to stand still

quiet, holding my breath
stopping time with your
ghostly touch
slowing the beating of my heart
until you fade away

strange happenings

the strangest thing happened
while driving home today
a song came on the radio
an old forgotten tune
but somehow the words
still tumbled from my lips
and filled my soul with a smile
i stopped at a red light
and glanced at the car
sitting quiet next to mine
a flash of brilliant light
my mind hesitated
and my heart clenched
as the world froze
except for your mouth
moving in time with the melody
of this song we shared
that moment always to be
and then the music faded
the light turned green
and the stranger drove away

chalkboard

if the mind were like a chalkboard
wouldn't life be so easy?
going through the tracks of time
with an oversized eraser
a little swipe here
and a big swipe there

if the mind were like a chalkboard
i'd jump right in
and pound my eraser against it
leaving behind oversized
white rectangles of dust
living life more childlike

if the mind were like a chalkboard
every now and again
a fingernail would scratch
against the memories
etched in the black
of my overcrowded mind

if the mind were like a chalkboard
wouldn't life be so easy?
i'd jump right in
and every now and again
i'd find a thought of you
and get out my oversized eraser

broken

you must enjoy
knowing i'm not
good enough for you
that i can never be
what you need
but i try, i really do

you must enjoy
rescuing the broken
taking in a lost
little kitten
feeding it and loving it
making it all yours

you must enjoy
all those nights alone
when i'm wandering
where i used to live
in the dark, in the night
without you, without you

you must enjoy
thinking it won't last
or maybe you do
and you don't care
i want it to work
but i just don't know

you must enjoy
knowing i'm not
good enough for you
that i can never be
what you need
but i try, i really do

near escape

driving down the highway
five hundred miles an hour in my mind
but only ninety according to the dash
the highway winds tossing my hair
but they can't blow away the past
through the open window
littering the roads with fear
harmony written for this moment
invades the confines of this car
a song that says everything
and does everything
except mention you by name
do you know what it's like
to have everything within your grasp
and still not realize the truth of it all
what a dilemma with which i now live
saying how i feel when no one's listening
and stumbling when everyone's watching
revealing the empty heart you left behind
must be the fifth one for you this week
and yet i still jumped into the fire
knowing and never once caring
i filled my days with the stars of the night
then rendered them broken and useless
now the darkness hovers, takes over my mind
in the end i'm left with no choice
but to run away as fast as i can

then again somehow i'm still here
and you never completely go away

throwaway

take this love, will you?
i didn't need it anyway
just lying around, doing nothing
serving no purpose
except to waste away the days

so take this love, will you?
it's pointless, useless
and i refuse to look at it anymore
surely it means something
to someone, somewhere

so take this love, will you?
intense and strong
i don't care where it goes
throw it away if you wish
i just don't want it here

alone

sitting alone
a single candle
burning slowly
flame dancing
smoke wafting

dreaming alone
dreaming of days
from yesterdays past
dreaming of days
yet to come

remembering alone
of sitting in a cemetery
that day i told you
how alone i was
without you

reliving alone
the words you spoke
the plans we made
the comfort of your touch
the feel of your mind

crying alone
over the changes in me
over the mysteries in you

how tragic it all was
and how it could never be

wishing alone
for no more confusion
grateful for the time we had
knowing it had to end
yet wanting the reason why

wondering alone
where my angel flies
with the grayest of wings
forever my protector
the lover of my soul

my mind, my heart, my soul
still screaming out a thousand times
i love you
but you do not hear
i do not want you to

so here i am
sitting alone
all alone
dreaming of you
dreaming you know me

one of those days

woke up desiring nothing but comfort
but my favorite shirt had a stain
found all my cigarettes were damp
but i haven't smoked in years

drifted outside for a little light
but the sun was on a coffee break
sought the cleansing of my life
but nature outright refused to rain

wanted some music to enlighten me
but the radio's songs resounded flat
sang all the notes left in my soul
but my entire world was off-key

removed the last of my chains
but ran into a room with hungry wolves
tried to jump off the nearest cliff
but i landed firmly on my feet

gave every last one of my dreams
in exchange for a single
...moment...
but my currency was refused

it's just one of those days
when all my rights

are flagged as wrongs
and all my wrongs are just that

one of those days
when life grins in my direction
as it shoves its ironies
up my backside

then i realize
the world turns
because of days like these
and suddenly i feel better

knowing i must be fueling the world
with all my days like this one
and that's my
selfless contribution

bleeding, broken
and stained
with a maniacal laugh on my lips
and a cynical smile on my heart

it all began with a kiss

it all began with a kiss
one stormy, summer night
on my back porch
under the sky
we gave the stars their light

it all began with a kiss
so gentle, soft, and true
i gave you my heart
my life and my soul
as into your world i flew

it all began with a kiss
then days turned into years
we fell in love
and when i cried
it was with joyful tears

it all began with a kiss
i knew together we could fly
but then one cold
dark winter's night
it all ended with goodbye

when the night comes

daylight is abundant
filling my soul with hope
dazing my way through life
a static smile on my face
but when the night comes
you suddenly appear
your voice, your laugh
a simple caress
the feel of you reinforces
the cracks in my heart
wetting my cheeks with
silent tears
i see you in a blur
out of focus
yet so perfectly formed
your rhythm defining me
moving, sweeping
but in the thick of the night
you're no more than a wisp
of a faded memory

waiting to fall

sometimes i feel as if there's nothing left to hold onto
a day, maybe two, and surely i'll be done
falling down, falling off, tumbling into oblivion
with nothing more than a broken heart to keep me safe
falling after a fall, there must be a better way to go
a trip and a stumble, those are easy to take
dropping down and losing my place, i've done those as well
but waiting to fall after i've fallen, that's no place to be

the road

an endless nightmare
floating naked through a mist
down that empty road
of tomorrow
i run and run
looking for something
somewhere
a sign, just one sign
shivering and shaking
fearful and tired
the road is so cold
so cold

for one moment
i want to dance in the fire
feel the warmth
of knowledge
and be hypnotized
by your mouth
held captive
in complete comfort
can't move, can't breathe
every thought stolen
i'm drifting away
higher and higher

my eyes fly open

and i'm back on the road
that empty road
of tomorrow
the dream gone
replaced by the reality
of the endless nightmare
of the nakedness
floating through the mist
shivering and shaking
the road is so cold
so cold

the puppeteer

how did you figure me out
i'm not what they're usually about
stumbling all over my pride
living that crazy kind of lie

always choosing to lose
almost wanting to be used
the pleasure and the pain
don't it all feel the same

it doesn't matter at all
if it hurts when i fall
pull me up, shove me down
let the happiness drown

hating to love and loving the hate
driving my soul to disastrous fate
veins flowing with nothing but strife
completely tied to my puppeteer's life

wrong way

hope comes in short bursts of flurries
melting in my eyes as it lands
and thoughts of you sting my soul
i try to ignore you
push you away and recede into the
safe depths of delusion

you were never really there
and even if you were you
it didn't mean a thing to me
never mattered one little bit
a flip of a switch, a blink of the heart
to drive you out, but

you're engraved in my mind
your music fills my being
runs through my veins
drags across my soul
a slow torment continually screaming
that you're no longer here

i never close my eyes
knowing i'll still see you
only discovering that the
curse of love is finding love
i'm always losing my mind knowing
i'm heading the wrong way

one more

just one more night
one restless night
turning in this tired bed
chasing elusive sleep

just one more mile
one endless mile
driving this broken vehicle
between white dashes of time

just one more song
one perfectly worded song
filling these deaf ears
with overplayed memories

just one more breath
one jagged breath
entering these shallow lungs
struggling to exhale

just one more tear
one lost, little tear
falling from these swollen eyes
following the river before it

just one more beat
one imploding beat

waking this bruised heart
reminding me of life

just one more kiss
one frantic, sensual kiss
stolen from this stranger's mouth
then i'll have forgotten you

brief love

The party is swankier than what I'm used to, so of course I'm dressed to the nines. At least that's what I thought before I left my house. Upon arriving at the party forty-five minutes ago, I realized that blowing a hundred dollars on a new top just wasn't enough to impress this crowd. Typically I'm not one to focus on appearance. Goodness knows I have spent more than my fair share of days with a naked face and rat's nest hair while still feeling good about life, but tonight I am claustrophobic in my own skin.

The moment we walked through the door of the downtown bar reserved for this soirée, Molly ditched me. That's typical of her. As opposed to my more casual apparel, Molly's backless, strapless, and immodest red dress seems to be the choice among the women here tonight. I know I'm the only woman in the room without a dress or a palette of makeup covering up faux tanned skin. For sanity's sake, I ignore the mass of bobbing implants lest I remember my parents were not kind in the passing of genes, although I briefly consider asking someone for a reference to their plastic surgeon.

I'm not sure why I agreed to come tonight. I know enough of the guests to make the night dreadful. I've also been to this bar enough times to know it's not quite up to the sophisticated standards of this lot. With Molly across the room surrounded by potential suitors, I'm free to explore the depths of a wine buzz and the instant wisdom that trails a few glasses. They're not serving Maker's Mark tonight, not at this pretentious gathering. I finish off my third glass of questionably tasting white wine whose name I can't pronounce even in the most sober state, and then I raise my glass at the bartender to order another of the same. Molly doesn't drink and is always proud to be my designated driver, even if it means a late night Taco Bell run fueled by my blissful intoxication.

Forty-five minutes into the party, standing at the bar with my fourth glass of almost undrinkable wine and I'm already a casualty of the night. Buzz riding high, I'm listening to Heath, a yuppie metrosexual wannabe, drone on about his job. My eyes flit about the room to see if anyone interesting is around. Anyone more interesting than Heath, that is. Not that I think I'm better than the man, but Heath is someone that I tolerate when there is no one else around willing to tolerate me.

Molly passes in my view. She throws up a slight and graceful wave in my direction, one that goes unnoticed by the gorgeous flesh on the other side of her. I shake my head at her, partly in disgust, mostly in admiration. In the five years I've known her, she's never altered her methods. Every few weeks she gets bored with her latest catch, and goes out to acquire a new piece of meat to look good on her arm, then keeps him around until he becomes replaceable. A quick once over of her latest treat tells me he may last three weeks if he's good. Then it's out the door, hit the road, later alligator.

Heath is still rambling in my direction, something about the accounts payable department. I don't even know where the guy works or what he does, but by the intensity in his voice, he thought he was saving the world. What scares me is that the man belongs to the same dating pool I do. He's lurking and waiting to find a woman to stay with him long enough so he can pollute the population with his little trolls.

I put the idea out of my head quickly, as I'm sure that one thought alone is enough to send me straight to hell. I nod and smile as Heath continues his monologue, then I turn my head to take one last desperate glance around the room.

My mouth falls open and I quickly clamp it closed before my jaw gets too close to the floor. The latest guy to enter the bar takes hold of my eyes without so much as glancing in my direction. He shakes hands with Jason, who could be Heath's twin, but unlike my impatience with Heath, this new man seems genuinely interested in Jason's one-sided conversation. If the man isn't interested in what Jason has to say, then he is certainly a most polite person and that only adds to the allure.

I calm myself, clear my thoughts, and block out all distractions so I can really take in the man. He's not gorgeous, not by Molly's standards, but I'm pulled toward him without moving a muscle. Blue shines across the room from mischievous eyes under a rough mass of dark hair. His face is a little more filled out than what I'm normally attracted to and under his button-down long-sleeved shirt, there is a slight protrusion. The guys I fall for are usually wiry and don't exceed 5'8. This giant of a man, who couldn't be even a slash of an inch under six feet, was definitely different for me. Of course at my age, the only guys who don't have a beer gut are musicians and I have strict rules about staying away from musicians. Past experiences and all.

The man's gaze wanders around the room, scoping the scene much as I have been doing ever since I ended up at the bar with Heath. Then his eyes do the unthinkable. They fall on me. Maybe it's because we're the only two people in the room dressed on the casual side, maybe it's because there was nowhere left for him to look, but something about me catches his eye and for the next few moments, I am the object of his focus. A corner of his mouth turns upward. I manage a smile and tear my eyes away to the floor. How could I be so dumb? To act like a shy schoolgirl after I flash what I know is the worst smile ever. No wonder I find myself spending my Saturday nights underdressed at swanky parties listening to guys like Heath.

Heath's voice scratches my ears and brings me round to reality like smelling salts. The last thing I want is this wondrous man who captures me so exquisitely to think I'm with the likes of Heath. I tell him I have to use the restroom. It's a viable excuse and perfect for weaseling my way out of a horrific conversation.

I make a conscious effort as I walk—not run—toward the restrooms in the back of the bar by the stage. The band is playing one of my favorite songs and as I get closer to the stage my hips involuntarily sway back and forth to the music. I try to stop them, but it's a natural phenomenon I am forced to live with. A few more drinks and I might be tempted to dance, but right now I simply want to open my bladder's floodgates and get another glass of wine to ease my current suffering.

I yank open the door to the bathroom and instantly regret the action. Momentum propels me forward into the invisible fog of stench resulting from too little cleanings and no proper ventilation system. I cough up a bit of bile into the back of my throat and my hand flies up to cover my mouth and nose. I pivot as quickly as my limbs allow and hastily vacate the bathroom. Time to get some more wine, just not at the bar Heath occupies.

As I consider my strategy to avoid Heath, I round the corner and run headfirst into the mystery man in the cramped hallway, bouncing off him like a trampoline. My joints tighten and all I can do is stare. He smiles at me and my body warms, releasing my bones into a limp mass.

"Excuse me." The words tumble out of my mouth in a sick and pathetically weak voice.

"No, my fault," the man replies. His voice isn't deep, but it isn't childish. Instead there is a hint of confidence hidden in the soothing tones that sound like warm milk as they flow into my ears and down into my veins. Three words and I already love his voice. I wonder what it sounds like in the dark.

I bite my bottom lip. It's a stupid habit, but I do it anyway because if I don't, I will say something I will surely regret later when I am alone in my bed. I move to the side to go around him and he moves to the same side. I try the other side and so does he. We stop trying to go around each other and laugh.

"I'm going that way," he says and points to his left. Then he points to his right. "You go that way."

I nod like an idiot because I am not allowed to talk like one. Not to this man.

"Unless of course you'd like to join me that way," he says with another smile and a sly wink.

Oh, he is killing me. Slowly, surely, and thoroughly killing me. I want to scream at him not to smile at me, not to talk to me, not to encourage my immature infatuation with him a second longer. If he does, my head and heart might both explode right here in this tiny bar hallway, and I don't think I'll stand a chance with him after that happens. Not that I have any chance with him now, but it's nice to hold onto little wisps of hope.

I point to his right and say, "I'm okay this way, thanks."

He smiles again and walks around me toward the men's restroom. I continue past the stage and into the main bar area. My mother must have dropped me on my head several times when I was a child, causing irreparable damage to the part of my brain that dictates how to act around an attractive person of the opposite sex. That's the only explanation for my words to him. Why am I cursed with this inability to flirt back? That's assuming, of course, that he was flirting with me. If he was, I'm sure he rapidly decided against any future flirting. I should have just let my head explode all over the walls in the hallway and saved myself this embarrassment.

I squeeze my way up to the bar, next to a couple of young girls out partying on daddy's trust fund, and flag down the bartender. Brian is a pretty cool guy, and he remembers me from the many other nights I've paid rent on one of his barstools.

"Sorry, lady," he yells in my direction. "No whiskey for you tonight."

"Yeah, what's up with that?" I scream back.

"They knew you were coming." He cracks an adorable smile. Truth be told, Brian's a guy you look forward to seeing, but you can't quite explain why. Too bad I don't know him better. His girlfriend is very lucky, I think.

"What will you have?" he asks me.

"White wine."

"What kind?" he probes, ever the patient and attentive bartender.

"Does it really matter?"

Brian simply nods and turns around to grab a wine glass. I stare at him while he artfully pours the wine, as I'm sure there is a proper way to do this and he's doing a damn fine job. He hands me the glass and I toss a couple of ones on the bar for him to keep. All the wine was paid for by our gracious host, but Brian still has to earn a living.

I clutch the stem in my hand and deliberately swirl the wine. The cyclone of liquid transfixes me, my eyes following the tiny sea in the bottom of the glass. I wonder what is happening in the molecules of this drink that causes some to follow it as a religion. I peek around at others at the bar to see if they are swirling their glasses, just to make sure I'm doing it right. My hand stutters and the wine splashes dangerously toward the rim. I'm sure that someone is watching me closely, ready to point me out as a phony to the rest of the crowd. Seasoned wine drinkers know when someone is faking it and tonight I'm sure they'd assume me a fraud. I certainly feel like one, swirling wine I hate around a pretentious glass while wearing this hundred-dollar top, trying to pretend I fit in with this bunch.

I stop the rush of liquid in the glass and take a drink. My taste buds revolt against the unwelcome flavor and I fight my instincts to bunch up my face in disgust. I see myself in the bar mirror and shudder at the sight of a girl who is not me. I'll return the top tomorrow and buy something more sensible. I lift the glass back to my lips and turn around to see if I can catch a glimpse of Molly.

I almost choke on the sip of wine. Mystery man is standing right behind me. I didn't hear him approach, didn't feel his presence. He's just suddenly there, an apparition of perfection that floated into my life, twice now. His large smile stops my heart and he peers directly into my soul with beautiful eyes.

"I wondered where you disappeared to," his magical voice says to me.

His words silence my world and I stop to consider what he means. He has been looking for me. Not Molly, not daddy's trust fund girls, but *me*. My heart goes into roller coaster mode, hitting four upside-down loops in a row. That, of course, awakens the butterflies in my stomach and arouses the woman in me.

With my internal organs in permanent disarray, a single neuron is somehow still firing away in my brain. "What are you drinking?" I ask, and my confidence spikes. Usually a line left for a guy to say, I regard the words that came from nowhere as a suave thing for me to utter.

His smile grows. "I wanted some Maker's, but for some reason this place refuses to be a real bar tonight."

My face goes deadpan and every part of me falls in love.

"I take it you don't like whiskey," he says to me.

I smile at him for the first time since I saw him across the room. "Actually I love the stuff. Maker's and 7 is my drink of choice."

He nods. "Mine, too." He leans in and whispers conspiratorially, "I'm not much for wine."

"It's the worst," I tell him. And then, because it's human nature to share anything that tastes bad with another person so we're not the only one suffering, I lift my glass and ask, "Wanna try some?"

He shrugs his shoulders and takes my glass. As he sips on the wine, my mind reels. Here is this amazing man whose name I don't even know and he's drinking from my glass of wine. Not from Molly's glass, not from one of the daddy's trust fund girl's glasses, but from *my* glass.

He makes a face that rivals one induced by bitter beer and hands the glass back to me. "I wonder if the red is any better," he comments.

I shake my head. I don't know if the red is better or not, but I don't want to ruin this moment by talking. I turn around to the bar and wave at Brian, who quickly answers my beckoning. "What can I do for you, darling?" he asks.

"Can I get a glass of white for my friend?"

Brian regards my new "friend" with a skeptical eye. He is looking out for me, which he usually does when I've had a few too many and my judgment is shot. I want to shout that I am not skewed by the awful tasting wine, but that I am, in fact, fully operational. No need to judge this one, my inner voice screams. He's way beyond the judgment of mere mortals. Brian doesn't outright reject my find of the night, but as my new companion hands him a large tip Brian gives him a stern glance that must mean something in guy code.

I turn to this stranger and raise my glass. His glass chinks against mine and we silently taste our wine. He winces. "It's not much better in my own glass."

A laugh rolls off my lips, but I stop when the staccato tones echo in my ears. I have a terrible laugh and I'm sure he thinks so, too.

Instead of whirling around and running for the door at the sound of my laugh, he keeps hold of my eyes with his and asks, "So what's your name?"

I hate the getting to know you stuff more than I hate my laugh. On average, I tell half my life story on the first date, which is about fifteen times a year. In return, I hear around fifteen partial life stories a year, sometimes the whole life story if they're a rambler like Heath. Then there's the thing about giving out your name in a bar. I give out far more fake names than my real name. I've been a lot of names with a lot of different occupations and life stories. Stacy, Anna, Danielle, Terri, Gina, Amy, Samantha.

"Claire," I tell this strange and wonderful man before me. It is not a lie. I've just taken my first step in being totally honest with him and it feels pretty okay.

"My grandmother's name was Claire," he says.

I don't take his revelation as a bad thing, but I really hope he liked his grandmother.

"A beautiful name," he adds, with a zinger of a smile.

"Thank you," I say with a gracefulness that doesn't belong to me. "What about you? Do you have a name?"

"Will."

I love it.

From over Will's shoulder, I see Molly directing a come hither wave at me. She's standing alone, and her motion is frantic. I give

Will a sheepish smile. "Um, can you wait here for a moment? My best friend, she, uh…" I point at Molly to finish my sentence.

Will turns his head to look at my gorgeous friend and turns back to me. "No problem. You're coming back, right?"

My lips form a genuine smile, the most genuine all night. He didn't run away to chase after Molly, as most men do the moment they see her. He only wanted to know if I would be back. "Absolutely," I answer. I hand him my glass as collateral.

I walk around him and start toward Molly, almost grateful for the distraction. These couple of moments away from Will can give me time to build up my resolve, strength, and game. This guy likes me. I may never be able to figure out why, but for tonight, this brief moment in the long span of life, that's the way it is.

For tonight. My smile drops with my self-esteem, as I push past a group of happy party-goers and continue on my path toward Molly. After tonight, after the terrible wine, things will be different with him. He'll remember that he's absolutely perfect and I'm a lesser creature and he'll snap out of it. There's no way that a man would ever find me attractive in any way, at least not for more than a couple of days. After that, once I'm fully in love with this man, he'll realize he made a mistake, he'll remember that he's looking for so much more than what I am, and he'll decide he's not willing to compromise. And while he'll walk away totally unscathed and with a sparkling new ego created by my foolishness and naivety, I will be on the edge of death.

I reach Molly and her bright eyes tell me she has met someone. I've seen that expression cross her face more than once. "What's going on?" I ask her.

"Ryan's meeting me at my place. Are you ready to go?"

Ryan must be the man I saw her with earlier. If he isn't, I'm sure he's equally as perfect. Molly would never settle for less.

I shift my glance toward Will. He's talking to Brian, oblivious to the insecurities that are controlling me. His head turns and he sees me. The smile on his lips lights its way across the room and touches my heart. Damn, he's beautiful. I watch Will resume his conversation with Brian and all my thoughts from earlier return. I look back to Molly.

"Were you talking with that guy over there?" Molly asks with a curious smile.

I shake my head in response to her question. I don't glance

behind me to make sure, but I assume Molly is following me as I make my way out the front door.

###

more by angie martin

The Boys Club

*Winner ~ Silver Medal for Suspense Fiction in the 2014 Reader's Favorite International Book Awards

Growing up a homeless juvenile delinquent left its mark on Gabriel Logan. He lived a throwaway existence until a former FBI agent recruited him for a fringe organization for boys like him, ones who could operate outside the law for the sake of justice. As an adult, he sets an example for the others and is slated to take over their group, until his work results in the murder of his pregnant wife.

Going through the motions of everyday life, Logan does only what's required of him with one goal in mind: kill Hugh Langston, the man responsible for his wife's death. When he's handed the opportunity to bring Langston down, he jumps at the chance, but the job will challenge him more than anything in the past. Not only does he have to save Langston's daughter from her father's hit list, but the job seems to have come to them a little too easily. Logan must find a way to not only rescue the one woman who can take down his biggest enemy, but also look into the men he trusts most to discover which one of them is betraying The Boys Club.

Reader Reviews for The Boys Club

"The Boys Club by Angie Martin is a brilliant read, and I highly recommend it to anyone seeking a bit of thriller and suspense." ~ Readers' Favorite

"There are no words that I could write that would even begin to do this book justice… It is just AMAZING!!! Go read it!! I highly recommend this book to anyone and everyone. It is that good!!" ~ Amazeballs Book Addicts

"Angie Martin brings her readers another jaw dropping story… that will leave you wanting more. Every chapter is filled with twist and turns that will have your heart racing…" ~ Fire and Ice Book Reviews

Conduit

How do you hide from a killer when he's in your mind?

Emily Monroe conceals her psychic gift from the world, but her abilities are much too strong to keep hidden from an equally gifted killer. A savvy private investigator, she discreetly uses her psychic prowess to solve cases. When the police ask her to assist on a new case, she soon learns the killer they seek is not only psychic, but is targeting her.

The killer wants more than to invade her mind; he wants her. Believing they are destined for each other, he uses his victims as conduits to communicate with her, and she hears their screams while they are tortured. She opens her mind to help the victims, but it gives him a portal that he uses to lure her to him. With the killer taking over her mind, she must somehow stop him before she becomes his next victim.

Reader Reviews for Conduit

"Conduit is a unique masterpiece…The amount of details given by the author and the wonderful way it was written causes heart pounding moments, fear of the dark and the need to check behind every closed door." ~ 5-star review from Amazon

"To say CONDUIT is a thriller is an understatement. From the first page to the harrowing conclusion, this is an absolute page-turner." ~ 5-star review from Amazon

"'Conduit' is an absorbing psychological thriller…which blends in more than a little splash of the paranormal as it gets underway with a suitably creepy and curious prologue setting the tone of the book and sinking claws of intrigue in from the word go." ~ 5-star review from Amazon

False Security

Rachel Thomas longs for normalcy, but if she stops running, she could die…or worse. Chased by a past that wishes to imprison her, haunted by dreams that seek to destroy her, Rachel finds solace in a love she could not predict. A love she cannot deter.

Mark Jacobson is the man who never needed love. He has his bookstore, his bachelorhood, and his freedom. In the moment he meets Rachel, he is swept into a world he didn't know existed. One filled with the purest of love. One filled with betrayal, lies, and murder.

Now Rachel and Mark are forced to face her past. The truth may kill them both.

Reader Reviews for False Security

"I HIGHLY recommend this book if you like suspense and surprises. Martin is a master at her craft and I cannot WAIT to read her next novel!" ~ 5-star review from Goodreads

"Ms. Martin had me rooting for Rachel and Mark… As danger escalated, I found it impossible to stop reading. A riveting story: if you enjoy romantic thrillers, you're in for a treat with 'False Security'." ~ 5-star review from Amazon

"False Security by Angie Martin is the kind of book I just couldn't stop reading. It's a new haunting love story…and this author knows how to get me hooked into a tale from the first page. There are…moments of beauty, quiet moments of love, and seething times of terror…False Security is a beautiful love story that you will not want to miss." ~5-star review from Amazon

"Excellent read for lovers of suspense thrillers." ~ 5-star review from Amazon

"…an emotionally gripping thriller." ~ The Wichita Eagle (review of 2004 release)

about angie martin

Angie is an award-winning, lifelong writer and firmly believes that words flow through her veins. She lives in Calimesa, California with her husband, two cats, and beloved dog. She also has two sons paving their own way in the world. She grew up in Wichita, Kansas and has lived all over the United States. Her work reflects her background in criminal justice and her love of Midwest life.

She has released three novels: "False Security" (romantic suspense), "Conduit" (paranormal, psychological thriller), and "The Boys Club" (suspense/thriller). She also has contributed short stories to anthologies.

"Conduit" won the Gold Medal for Paranormal Fiction in the 2014 Readers' Favorite International Book Awards. "The Boys Club" won the Silver Medal for Suspense Fiction in the 2015 Readers' Favorite International Book Awards. It was also voted as one of the 2014-15 Top 50 Self-Published Books Worth Reading (ReadFree.ly). All of her works have won additional readers' choice and blog choice awards.

Angie's Books: bit.ly/thrillingbooks

Website: www.angiemartinbooks.com

Fan group: www.facebook.com/groups/angiesconduits

Facebook: www.facebook.com/authorangiemartin

Twitter: www.twitter.com/zmbchica

one last thing

Thanks for reading! If you enjoyed this book, I'd be very grateful if you would post a short review on Amazon and/or Goodreads. Your support really does make a difference and I read all the reviews personally so I can get your feedback. Thank you again for your support!